HAMBURGERS

by Golriz Golkar

Cody Koala

An Imprint of Pop!
popbooksonline.com

abdobooks.com
Published by Pop!, a division of ABDO, PO Box 398166, Minneapolis,
Minnesota 55439. Copyright © 2019 by POP, LLC. International copyrights
reserved in all countries. No part of this book may be reproduced in any
form without written permission from the publisher. Pop!™ is a trademark
and logo of POP, LLC.

Printed in the United States of America, North Mankato, Minnesota

082018
012019

THIS BOOK CONTAINS
RECYCLED MATERIALS

Cover Photo: Shutterstock Images
Interior Photos: Shutterstock Images, 1, 5 (top), 5 (bottom left), 5 (bottom
right), 6, 9, 12, 13, 16, 19 (bottom left), 19 (bottom right), 21; Education Images/
Universal Images Group/Getty Images, 11; iStockphoto, 15, 19 (top)

Editor: Charly Haley
Series Designer: Laura Mitchell

Library of Congress Control Number: 2018949238
Publisher's Cataloging-in-Publication Data

Names: Golkar, Golriz, author.
Title: Hamburgers / by Golriz Golkar.
Description: Minneapolis, Minnesota: Pop!, 2019 | Series: Favorite foods |
    Includes online resources and index.
Identifiers: ISBN 9781532161896 (lib. bdg.) | ISBN 9781641855600 (pbk) | ISBN
    9781532162954 (ebook)
Subjects: LCSH: Hamburgers--Juvenile literature. | Foods--Juvenile
    literature. | Children's eating habits--Juvenile literature. | Food
    preferences--Juvenile literature.
Classification: DDC 641--dc23

Hello! My name is

Cody Koala

Pop open this book and you'll find QR codes like this one, loaded with information, so you can learn even more!

Scan this code* and others like it while you read, or visit the website below to make this book pop.

popbooksonline.com/hamburgers

*Scanning QR codes requires a web-enabled smart device with a QR code reader app and a camera.

Table of Contents

Chapter 1

From Germany

German **immigrants** sailed to America in the 1840s. On their ship, they ate **ground** beef mixed with spices. The food was popular in Hamburg, Germany.

Watch a video here!

In America, the Germans opened grocery stores and restaurants. Soon, many people were eating "Hamburg steak." The food later became known as hamburger.

Chapter 2

Here Comes the Bun

The hamburger became a sandwich in 1900. A restaurant in Connecticut served ground beef between two slices of toast.

Learn more here!

These sandwiches were featured at the 1904 Saint Louis World's Fair. Everyone started calling them hamburgers. The food became popular across America.

In 1916, Walter Anderson
invented the first round
hamburger bun.

Then he opened the
first **chain** of hamburger
restaurants, White Castle.
White Castle restaurants still
exist today.

Chapter 3

Hamburgers Today

Hamburgers became a popular **fast food** in the 1950s. They were served quickly and could be eaten at home.

Learn more here!

Today, hamburgers are eaten all over the world. Chain restaurants such as McDonald's and Burger King are found in many countries.

Americans eat more than 40 billion hamburgers every year.

Chapter 4

How to Make a Hamburger

With help from an adult, you can make hamburgers at home! First, take some ground beef. Form it into a **patty**. Make the patty flat and round.

Complete an activity here!

Add salt and pepper. Then fry or grill the patty. Cook each side. Put the burger on a bun. Add lettuce, tomato, cheese, or your favorite toppings.

The biggest burger ever made weighed almost 1,800 pounds. That's how much a giraffe weighs!

Hamburger Ingredients

- Ground beef
- Salt
- Pepper
- Bun

Toppings:
- Cheese
- Ketchup, mayonnaise, or mustard
- Lettuce
- Onions
- Pickles
- Tomato

Making Connections

Text-to-Self

Do you like to eat hamburgers? What is your favorite food?

Text-to-Text

Have you read any other books about food? What did you learn?

Text-to-World

Hamburgers came from a food that German people brought to America. What other popular American foods are from other countries?

Glossary

chain – many businesses of the same kind, owned by the same company.

fast food – restaurant food that is made and served quickly.

ground – chopped or crushed into very small pieces.

immigrant – a person who moved from another country.

patty – a small, flat, round piece of meat.

Index

Online Resources

popbooksonline.com

Thanks for reading this Cody Koala book!

Scan this code* and others like it in this book, or visit the website below to make this book pop!

popbooksonline.com/hamburgers

*Scanning QR codes requires a web-enabled smart device with a QR code reader app and a camera.